DYI Household H

Your Guide On How To Save Massive Time, Energy and Money & Make Life Easier

<u>155 tips + 41 recipes</u>

My Mailing list: If you would like to **receive new Kindle reads** on **weight loss, wellness, diets, recipes and healthy living** for FREE I invite you to my Mailing List. Whenever my new book is out, I set the free period for two days. You will get an e-mail notification and will **be the first to get the book for $0** during its limited promotion.

Why would I do this when it took me countless hours to write these e-books?

First of all, that's my way of saying **"thank you"** to my new readers. Second of all – **I want to spread the word about my new books and ideas.** Mind you that **I hate spam and e-mails that come too frequently** - no worries about that.

If you think that's a good idea and are in, just follow this link:

http://eepurl.com/6elQD

Introduction

In our fast changing lives, it's all about convenience. Whether it is the food we eat or the products we use, everything has become commercial. When we say commercial, the stress is on pointing out that there is a severe death of natural and healthy products and commodities in our lives.

There is just so much toxicity around; from the air we breathe, to the food we eat and the things we use that we unknowingly are inviting a lot of diseases and other health issues in our lives.

As the adage 'where there is a will, there is a way' goes, if you decide to take matters in your hands, you will realize that it is not so difficult to adapt healthy living. One major change that you can bring about in your life is to say "no" to commercial cleaning products (which are known to be toxic) and replacing them with natural, healthy and so often more effective homemade cleaners.

If you manage to do this, you will ensure that you keep the toxicity of commercial cleaning products out of your life and build a safe and healthy environment for yourself and your family.

This is exactly what I wish to communicate through this book, as I bring across some smart cleaning hacks and recipes for cleaning products that you can make from the comforts of your home. Rather than running to the departmental store and buying substandard cleaning products that can cause allergies and too many other problems, it is time you easily start making these natural cleaners on your own.

Through this book, you can learn several tips and tricks to keep your house clean through homemade cleaning hacks, and avoid the hassle of buying expensive cleaning products.

This book is designed to enlighten you with several easy house cleaning hacks, which are simple in their approach, yet deliver brilliant results every single time. With just a few household items and commonly found ingredients like lime, vinegar, essential oils, hydrogen peroxide, salt, baking powder etc., you can achieve great results that even commercial (read expensive) products cannot deliver.

So what are we waiting for? Let's start reading up on these marvelous tips and tricks!

Chapter 1: The Truth About Cleaning

First and foremost, thank you for buying this book and I assure you, by the time you are done reading, not only will you be raring to try out the various hacks and notions we have mentioned; but also have your besties on call to gloat about how good the tips really are.

All the hacks and recipes mentioned in the book have been personally tested and the results have always been great.

What prompted me to go all natural and make my own recipes, is the fact that commercial products these days are not only expensive, but also laden with so many chemicals. They end up doing more harm than good. It was; therefore, imperative to make skin and pet friendly cleaning products at home, to safeguard my family's health, while saving massive money and time simultaneously.

Yes, there are also various hacks that will cut short the time you spend cleaning your house; time that you can spend with family and friends. Not only will the recipes and hacks help you save on time and energy, they also give you the satisfaction of having done your bit for the conservation of the environment. You will be surprised how many effective, cheap and harmless cleaning products you already own in your household!

It is, however, important to do patch tests and try out some of the recipes on a small area to see the reaction. If it does not have any adverse reaction then you can use it to clean the entire item.

All the recipes are easy to make and on a scale of 1 to 5 difficulty level, most figure well within the 1-3 range.

I'm sure, by now you must be eager to read up and try out these hacks to beautify your house naturally.

Go on then, let us begin!

Chapter 2: Easy Bathroom Cleaning Hacks

I have decided to start off by introducing you to bathroom cleaning hacks, since bathrooms and toilets are places that need the maximum amount of cleaning. They tend to get greasy all too easy and accumulate a lot of grime owing to their constant exposure to oils, soap, scum and dirt. There are four areas in the bathroom that require the maximum amount of cleaning viz. tiles, commode, faucets & mirrors and shower & bathtub. Let us now look at each one in detail.

Hacks to keep the tiles clean

White, green, blue, pink, beige or black; - no matter the color of the tiles, by the end of the week, they all pretty much get covered in brownish mildew. Also known as mold, it is a type of fungus that grows on damp surfaces. On the surface, it may seem easy to clean off, but the grout in between the tiles can be a nightmare. Apart from being an eye sore, they are highly capable of causing illnesses that can harm you and your family. It is; therefore, important to keep bathrooms tiles clean and sparkly.

Tips:-

- To clean the surface of the tiles, use a sponge dipped in vinegar and rub until all the mildew is wiped off. Maintaining a circular motion will help in speeding up the process.

- The worst part of cleaning tiles can be cleaning the gaps in between them. Using a toothbrush or a q-tip and rubbing vinegar on them can help loosen the grout.

- Use cooking spray to remove soap scum. Spray a little cooking spray over the tiles and allow it to cut through the grease. Wipe it off using a wet sponge.

- Rubbing white tiles with orange or lemon peels can help in keeping them white. You can instead spray water that is boiled with lemon peels and allow it to stand overnight. Wipe it off using a sponge dipped in warm water.

- To prevent shaving cream bottles and other metallic surface from causing rust and develop stains on the tiles, apply a thin coat of clear nail polish at the bottom of the cans.

Recipes

Tile scrub
Ingredients

- 1 cup kosher salt or rock salt

- 1 cup Baking powder

- ½ cup Borax powder

Preparation

1. Combine all the ingredients and store in a plastic jar.

2. Sprinkle some of the mixture on a sponge and scrub tiles.

3. The salt and soda will help scrub away the dirt and mildew, while the borax will help in bleaching.

Note: Use gloves while using the borax powder as it can burn your skin.

Tile cleaner

Ingredients

- 4 cups baking soda

- 1 cup kosher salt

- 1 cup vinegar

- 3 cups water

- 1 cup hydrogen peroxide (35% strength)

- Spray bottle

Preparation

1. Mix the soda and salt together and store in a jar.

2. In a spray bottle, pour the vinegar, water and hydrogen peroxide and give it a shake.

3. At the time of cleaning, spray the tiles generously with the vinegar mixture and allow it to stand for a minimum of 30 minutes and a maximum of 12 hours (overnight).

4. The next morning, use a sponge or toothbrush to rub the salt mix over and in between the tiles. Use warm water to spray it off.

Note: Use gloves while working with the hydrogen peroxide, as it can irritate the skin.

Tile cleaner II
Ingredients:

- 4 cups of baking soda
- 8 teaspoons of vegetable glycerin
- 1 cup of liquid castile soap (get the one without Diethanolamine (DEA) or sodium lauryl sulfate (SLS)).
- 10 drops of antibacterial essential oil (any scent – tea tree, lavender, rosemary, etc.).

Preparation:

1. Mix all the ingredients mentioned above. Pour the solution in a glass jar and seal it. well.
2. Use it by pouring it over the area you wish to clean. It is effective on tiles, kitchen counters etc.

Note: This solution has a shelf life of nearly two years. If you wish to store a dry scrub instead of a liquid one, make soft dry scrubs by simply mixing it with salt or baking soda. You can also use a mixture of the two with essential oils of your favorite scent (about 12-15 drops).

Grout remover

Ingredients

- 1 cup Vinegar

- 1 cup Dish liquid (preferably lemon scented)

Preparation

1. Mix the vinegar and dish liquid together and store in a bottle.

2. Spray between the tiles or dip a toothbrush into the mix and scrub between the tiles.

3. Spray with a jet spray of water.

Hacks to keep the washbasin/commode clean

A clean bowl will not only make you feel good about entering your bathroom but also safeguard your health against various diseases.

Commodes are some of the nastiest of places in the house that can get dirty in no time at all. Maintaining clean and sparkly bowls can pose quite the challenge. It may seem impossible to clean without using commercial cleaning products. That; however, is not true. Homemade hacks can work just as well.

Let's now look at tips to keep the bowl clean and recipes to make homemade toilet cleaners.

Tips:-

- Toilet bowls can develop rust around the sitting area. Using a pumice stone with a long handle can help in removing the rust by scrubbing it away.

- Coca-Cola makes for a great toilet cleaner! Just pour in a bottle (small or medium, depending on the size of the commode) and let it stand overnight. Use a brush to clean the inside and flush.

- Pouring mouthwash into the toilet will not just help in cleaning it but also kill the germs in it. Allow the mouthwash to stand in it overnight.

- Cleaning the areas around and at the base of the commode can be a nightmare. You can spray an equal combination of vinegar and hot water around the outlet pipe and at the base of the commode and let it rest overnight. Using a toilet brush, scrub the vinegar sprayed area and spray hot water.

- Making a paste of lemon and soda, applying it around the base and cleaning it with vinegar can help get rid of tough stains.

- Dropping a couple of Alka-Seltzer or Pepto-Bismol tablets into the commode and flushing immediately with warm water can help in unclogging them.

- Use tissues to wipe the outside of the bowl using a couple of drops of baby oil. That will allow the bowl to remain shiny.

- After using the toilet brush, allow it to drip by placing it between the seat cover and bowl. That way, the brush can dry completely before going back into its holder.

Recipes for commode cleaners

Cleaning liquid

Ingredients

- 1 cup vinegar

- 15 drops essential oil (rose, lavender etc.)

Preparation

1. Place the vinegar and essential oils in a bottle and give it a good shake.

2. Pour it into the bowl and let it remain overnight.

3. Scrub it using a brush and flush.

Flush bombs

Ingredients

- 1 cup baking soda

- 1 cup citric acid crystals

- 30 drops essential oil

- Witch hazel spray (optional)

Preparation

1. Mix all the ingredients in a glass bowl and make small balls out of the mixture.

2. Place each ball in a holder (ice cube tray) and spray each with witch hazel.

3. Place one bomb inside the flush tank every morning.

4. Although the first flush will flush out most of the bomb, the subsequent flushes will still smell fresh.

Toilet disinfectants
Ingredients:

- 2 teaspoons sodium borate (borax)
- ¼ teaspoon castile soap (liquid)
- 4 tablespoons distilled white vinegar
- 4 cups boiling water

Preparation:

1. Take a container or spray bottle and pour all the above ingredients in it. Mix well.
2. Dip a cloth in the solution or spray the liquid on the surface you want to disinfect and wipe.
3. You can also soak the cleaning sponge in this solution to clean it, or let it stay in your kitchen dustbin.
4. This mixture can be used to clean cabinet corners or tap handles too.

Rust remover

The area near the faucets, under the sink or near the commode may develop rust stains due to the constant reaction between metal fixtures and water. They cannot be removed with ordinary cleaners but they are not that stubborn either. Use the following recipe to make a rust remover.

Ingredients:

- Kosher salt
- Lime

Preparation:

1. Sprinkle the salt exactly over the rust stains.
2. Cut a lime into halves, and squeeze it over the salt (enough for the salt to be soaked up in it).
3. Let it stay for at least 2-3 hours.
4. Use the rinds that are left after squeezing to scrub over the rust marks. Use slight pressure if the rust does not come off easily.

Hacks to keep the faucets & mirrors clean

Faucets and mirrors can stain very easily and can be extremely tough to clean. Putting your hand on messy taps may seem disgusting and you may not want to operate them at all. It is; therefore, important to clean taps and maintain them that way.

Tips:-

- Use vinegar to clean the taps. Dip a toothbrush in vinegar and rub the surface of the taps. The vinegar breaks down the tough dirt and allows it to fall off.

- Tying a plastic bag containing vinegar around the tap and allowing it to remain overnight can help in cleaning away the hard water stains.

- Rubbing a lemon wedge on the taps can render them sparkly and clean.

- To prevent unsightly finger prints from appearing on taps, simply rub some wax paper all over them.

Recipes

Faucet cleaner (to remove hard water stains)
Ingredients

- Vinegar

- Baking soda

Preparation

1. Mix a little baking soda with vinegar and bring it to a pasty consistency.

2. Use a toothbrush to apply the paste on a tap and scrub it on the hard water stains.

3. After the unsightly stains start to loosen, use a jet of water to help them fall off.

Faucet cleaner II
Ingredients

- 1 Grapefruit
- 1/4 cup coarse kosher salt

Preparation:

1. Take a grapefruit and cut it into two halves. One grapefruit is enough to clean up the entire bath or shower including the faucets.
2. Cover the exposed side of the half cut grapefruit with a thick layer of kosher salt.
3. With the remaining salt, sprinkle over the bottom of the bathtub.
4. Scrub the surface of the bathtub using the grapefruit. Make sure that you slightly squeeze the grapefruit while rubbing, so that the citrus juice covers the surface. Use the rind to rub over more stubborn areas.
5. Rinse off the dirt that falls off and the bits of the fruit with water.

Hacks to clean mirrors

Bathroom mirrors are meant to be clean and shiny in order to serve their true purpose, of reflecting your image. However, they more often than not turn hazy, develop spots and also start losing their shiny quality. Here are some ways in which you can clean your mirrors and maintain them well.

Tips:-

- Mirrors can be cleaned using newspapers. Cut them into small strips and rub the surface of the mirror in preferably just one direction viz.

start from left to right and rub it in one stroke. Then lift and repeat. A great idea is to also buy a streak-free mirror/glass cleaning cloth. It is also great for making metal and glass parts or your oven shiny.

- Wipe the surface of the mirror by rubbing alcohol to get rid of toothpaste stains, creams, soap scum, hairspray etc. Soak small cotton balls in the alcohol and use them to rub the mirrors.

- A concoction of baking soda and vinegar can be used to keep streaks away.

- Apply shaving cream or foam on the entire length of the mirror and wipe it using a roll of paper. This will prevent the mirror from fogging up after a hot shower.

- Rubbing toothpaste over scratches can help in covering them.

Recipe for cleaning glass and mirror

Glass cleaner
Ingredients:

- 1/4 cup isopropyl (rubbing) alcohol
- 1/4 cup white vinegar (you may also try apple cider vinegar)
- 1 tablespoon cornstarch (to reduce streaks on the glass)
- 8-10 drops of essential oil (try the citrus scent like lemon, or orange. You can also opt for lavender, rosemary, tea tree etc.)
- 2 cups water

Preparation:

1. Mix all the ingredients mentioned above and store in a spray bottle.
2. Spray the mixture on the glass surface of the bathroom window or glass partitions.
3. Wipe it off using a damp cloth or sponge, all strokes in the same direction. (Do not use any cloth which is furry or might leave bits of threads sticking on to the surface.)

Note: If you are using this solution to clean a window, make sure you don't do it under direct sunlight. This will cause the stains to remain on the glass and the wipe marks may also be visible.

Hacks to keep the shower & bathtub clean

Isn't it ironic that showers are supposed to keep us clean and while doing so, end up dirtying themselves? Shower areas and bathtubs get dirty very quickly and might require cleaning on a daily basis. But nobody has the time for that these days. Hence, it is important to know a few handy hints and hacks to help clean it thoroughly enough to keep it hygienic for at least a week.

Tips:-

- Vinegar helps in getting rid of rust stains. Pour some on the stains and let it stand for at least half an hour. Then scrub using steel wool.

- Pour vinegar in a plastic cover and place it around the shower head. You can also detach the shower head and place it inside the plastic bag and let it remain in there overnight. All the dirt and hard water stains will separate from the shower head.

- Fill the tub with a little water and a cup of sea salt. Immerse the entire shower curtain in it and allow it to soak for 30 minutes. Remove and hang the curtain. Doing so will prevent mildew and mold from growing on the curtains.

- Bathtub rings can be unsightly. To prevent their occurrence, pour a few drops of baby oil every time you get into the tub.

- If you already have stains then run a dryer over them. Dryers tend to loosen the grease - but be very careful while doing so. No water allowed!

- To clean the washing machine, just pour in 4 cups vinegar and 1 cup baking soda. Run a hot water cycle and your machine will be as good as new.

Recipe for bathroom cleaners

Bathtub scrub
Ingredients

- 1 cup kosher salt

- 1 cup baking soda

- Vinegar

Preparation

1. Mix the salt and soda together and store in a jar.

2. Use it to scrub the tub once a week making sure to scrub away all built up grime and dirt.

Vodka mix
Ingredients

- 1 bottle vodka

- 10 drops of rose essence

Preparation

1. Mix the vodka and rose essence together and store in a jar.

2. Pour it inside the tub and let it stay for 30 minutes. The vodka breaks down dirt and grime and the essence renders a pleasant fragrance.

3. Wash off with ample water.

Bathroom mold remover
Ingredients:

- Hydrogen peroxide (3% concentration solution)
- Water

Preparation:

1. Pour 3% hydrogen peroxide in a jar and add twice the amount of water. (Make the final quantity according to the area that needs to be cleaned.)
2. Pour the mix into a bottle. Mix well and spray it over the moldy areas in the bathroom.
3. Let it stay for at least an hour.
4. Use a jet of water/hand spray to rinse off the mold.

Easy homemade disinfectant wipes

Ingredients

- 4-5 4x4 soft cloth pieces

- 1 cup water

- 2 tablespoons vinegar

- 2 tablespoon castile soap (or dish liquid)

- 10 drops tea tree oil

Preparation

1. Place the pieces of cloths stacked on top of each other and pressed down.

2. Mix all the ingredients in a bowl and pour on the topmost cloth and wait for it to permeate through and soak even the bottom-most cloth.

3. Use to wipe flush knobs, counters, wash basins etc.

Note:-Run hot water taps for ten minutes with windows and doors closed and allow enough steam to accumulate. The steam makes cleaning much easier. It is a good idea to clean the bathroom just after a shower.

Bathroom fresheners

Bathrooms are one of the most unhygienic and smelliest parts of your home. For a fresh and pleasant smelling bathroom, use the following recipes.

Ingredients:

- Essential oil (any scent of your choice)
- Distilled water

Preparation:

1. Take a spray bottle and fill it with water. Add about 50 – 60 drops of essential oil.
2. You can also mix different essential oils to get the desired fragrance.
3. Spray the mixture in all the corners of your bathroom.

Note: For a calming effect, you can mix 30 drops of lavender essential oil, 10 drops of chamomile essential oil with 10 drops of rosemary essential oil.

For a peppier and mood uplifting smell, try this combination: ¾ teaspoon lavender essential oil with 1 teaspoon orange essential oil and ½ teaspoon lemon essential oil. This mixture has a fruity and citrus smell.

Laundry cleaning

After if you have cleaned every nook and corner of your bathroom, and everything is shining and sparkling, it is time to deal with the big bundle of laundry. You can make your own non-toxic detergent by following the simple steps. This will also help you to maintain the whiteness of your whites.

Recipe for laundry detergent
Ingredients:

- 4 cups soap flakes
- 2 cups baking soda
- 1 cup sodium bicarbonate (washing soda)
- 1-2 tablespoon oxygen bleach (optional, for extra whitening power)

Preparation:

1. To make soap flakes, grate a vegetable soap of your choice using a kitchen grater..
2. Mix all these ingredients together in a glass container and store.
3. While washing laundry, use 1 tablespoon of the detergent per load of laundry. If the laundry is heavily soiled or if the load is heavy, use 2 tablespoons of the detergent.
4. Wash in cold or warm water.

Note: For a whitening effect, try hydrogen peroxide as opposed to bleach. For fabric softener, add a cup of distilled white vinegar. For dull whites, soak them in the washer for about 30 minutes. Add half a cup of 3% peroxide to it.

Laundry spot remover

Ingredients:

- 1 and 1/2 cups of water
- 1/4 cup liquid vegetable glycerin
- 1/4 cup liquid castile soap
- 5-10 drops of lemon essential oil

Preparation:

1. Mix all the above mentioned ingredients in a glass spray bottle or a plastic squeeze bottle. (If your mixture contains any citrus essential oil, it is advisable to store the mixture in a glass spray bottle as the citrus can react with the plastic. If you skip the essential oil, then a plastic squeeze bottle will do.)
2. Shake the bottle properly before use. Apply the mixture over the spots on the fabric and rub it with your fingertips.
3. Let it stay for some time, like an hour or so, before cleaning with the laundry.

Note: Like most cleaners, the mixture works best if it is applied immediately (when the stain is fresh). This mixture may not work well on spots that have already been washed once. Also, if you fear that it might cause discoloration, it is advisable that you check it once in an inconspicuous area of the fabric, though the chances of this are very slim.

Chapter 3: Kitchen Cleaning Hacks

In the previous chapter, we looked at easy bathroom cleaning hacks that you can use to keep your restrooms clean, gleaming and fresh smelling. Let us now look at simple kitchen cleaning hacks, that will make you want to spend more time there and cook gourmet meals for your family or friends.

The seven main areas that need cleaning in the kitchen are-counter tops, cabinets, the sink, stove or grill top, appliances, kitchen dustbins and utensils.

Hacks for cleaning counter tops

Counter and table tops get soiled very easily, as they are used for so many things including chopping, storing condiments, storing utensils, placing appliances etc. etc.

Here are some tips and hacks to keep counter and table tops clean.

Tips:-

- Granite counter tops are fairly common and despite their natural quality of having a shiny surface, they can easily lose their sheen. Rubbing alcohol is a great idea that can be used to get rid of food and condiment stains from granite surfaces without causing them to lose their sheen.

- Mix equal parts of rubbing alcohol and warm water. Dip a sponge in the mixture and give the counter top a good scrub. That will help in getting rid of all types of stains including rust stains.

- Baking soda is great to not just clean and remove stains but also deodorize the surface. Mix half a cup of baking soda with two cups of water and use a sponge to dip and wipe the counter top. The soda will get rid of tough food stains and also help in removing odors left behind by condiments.

- If you are stuck with a very tough stain, like coffee mug rings that have completely dried out, then you can make a dense mixture of baking soda & water and apply it over the stains. Let it rest overnight. The next morning use a wet sponge to rub over the stains.

- Sometimes the best tip is to clean away grease using more grease. Just scrub the surface of the greased wall or tile using mineral oil. The mineral oil will loosen and remove the grease stains easily.

Recipes

Counter cleaning liquid
Ingredients

- 1 cup hydrogen peroxide (35% strength)

- 1 cup water

Preparation

- Mix the hydrogen peroxide and water together and place in a spray bottle.

- Spray the mixture over table and counter tops and wipe using a sponge or dryer sheets.

- This spray can be used on any surface including marble, granite, wood etc.

Note:-Do not use any form of citric acid for cleaning marble and granite tops as they can strip the surface off of their sheen for good.

Cleaning cutting board

Ingredients:

- 1 large lemon
- 1 teaspoon rock/kosher salt

Preparation:

1. This one takes no preparation as such. Simply sprinkle any coarse salt on the surface of the cutting board, preferable kosher salt.
2. Cut a lemon into halves and rub one half of it on the surface of the board.
3. Let it sit for 10 minutes and then wash it off with warm water. This will clean, as well as sanitize the cutting board.

The handiest tool that can be used to scrape away dry stains and other dirt on a cutting board is a painter's scrapper. The tool can be used to scrap away any stain with just a single stroke.

Hacks for cleaning kitchen cabinets

From cereal boxes to pasta sauces, kitchen cabinets and pantries are used to store a whole variety of foods. And with such variety comes a whole world of spills and stains.

Stains that are present inside cabinets are not just unsightly but can also start developing mold, if not cleaned on time. Here are some tips and hacks to clean kitchen cabinets from the inside out.

Tips:-

- Kitchen cabinet doors have the tendency of developing a thick grimy surface, which then starts accumulating hair and animal fur. Not only can they be unsightly but also stick to hands while operating the doors. One good way of getting rid of that grime is by scrubbing it using equal quantities of baking soda and mineral oil mixed together. Use a toothbrush to scrub the surface with the mixture.

- The same paste can be used to clean the insides of the cupboard as well.

- Use vinegar to wipe the insides of the cabinet. Vinegar helps get rid of sauce and stains of liquids that have dried out. Make a mixture of equal parts vinegar and water and add in a few drops of orange essential oil to make the liquid smell good.

- Mix 50% vinegar and 50% liquid soap to make the best tile grease remover. Especially the tiles placed right above the stove.

- The handiest tool that can be used to scrap away dried stains and other dirt is a painter's scrapper. The tool can be used to scrap away any stain with just a single stroke.

- Mix 50% rubbing alcohol and 50% water, and spray it inside the entire length and breadth of the cupboard or cabinet. Clean off with a dry sponge. This will prevent the buildup of germs and also keep ants and other insects at bay.

Recipe

Cleaning kitchen cabinet

Ingredients:
- Rubbing Alcohol
- Water

Preparation

- Mix 50% rubbing alcohol and 50% water, and spray it inside the entire length and breadth of the cupboard or cabinet.
- Clean off with a dry sponge. This will prevent the buildup of germs and also keep ants and other insects at bay.

Hacks for Cleaning the Sink

Cleaning sinks can be a nightmare! Clogged up sinks not only stink but also cause unhygienic water to spill out and dirty the floor. It is, therefore imperative, to maintain a clean, dry, unclogged sink.

Tips:-

- Sinks are generally made of stainless steel and the best way to clean a dirty sink is by sprinkling about half a cup of baking powder and letting it rest for around 5 to 7 minutes. Then use a toothbrush or a scrubber and scrub until all stains are removed. Make sure that the sink is dry before sprinkling in the baking powder.

- An alternative to that method is to sprinkle sea salt and squeeze in a lemon. The lemon and salt work together to break the bond between the stains on the surface of the sink. Rub using a toothbrush until all stains are removed. Spray with warm water. You can also use a lemon rind to rub the salt into the sink.

- The best trick to unclog a clogged sink is to drop Alka-Seltzer tablets into it. The pills start to dissolve and help ease out the clogging substance out of the drainage system.

- For porcelain sinks, use a combination of baking soda and hydrogen peroxide. Scrub the insides of the sink using the combination and finish off with an application of lemon oil.

- To clean vegetables and fruits, clog the sink and fill it up with water and add a few drops of vinegar. Allow the fruits and veggies to soak in it for 10 minutes.

Recipe

Cleaning the sink

Ingredients:

- 1 cup salt
- water (1.6 gallons, 6 liters)
- 1 cup baking soda
- 1 cup vinegar

Preparation:

1. For a light drain cleaner, mix the salt in 6 liters of water.
2. If your drain is too clogged, then pour half a cup of baking soda down the drain, followed by half a cup of vinegar. This solution is a stronger cleaner.
3. Let it stay for 15 minutes. The reaction between the baking soda and vinegar will clean the drain.
4. Pour hot water down the drain to clean the residue.

Note: This method is best suited for drains made of metal. Plastic pipes may melt due to hot water. Keep the water and salt solution lukewarm or according to the heat resistance of your plastic pipe.

Also, if you have used a commercial drain opener, then do not use vinegar to clean further. This might lead to the creation of dangerous fumes.

Hacks to clean the stove top/grill

Stove tops suffer the most amount of damage in the kitchen. From black soot to dried up pasta sauce, the stove top goes from clean to greasy in no time at all.

Dry food stains have the tendency of heating up and burning, causing for a burnt smell to waft throughout the house. This is especially embarrassing, when you have guests over. Here are tips to avoid those situations and maintain a clean stove top.

Tips:-

- Remove the rings from the burner top and place it inside a plastic bag containing ammonia. Place about half a cup of ammonia and it is not necessary for the burners to be immersed in it. Remove and wipe with a wet sponge the next morning.

- Alternately, boil water and add about 2 to 3 handfuls of baking soda in the same and give it a good mix. Drop in the rings and let them remain in the solution overnight. You can also clean electric stove coils the same way.

- Scrub the rest of the stove using a combination of baking soda and water. Using a toothbrush, scrub the stove, making sure to remove as much stains as possible.

- For ceramic stove tops, use a scrapper to scrap away the black soot and use a mixture of baking soda and vinegar to clean it.

- Use a sponge or clean cloth to polish stove tops using your car polish. The car polish will not just help it shine, but also allow for easier cleaning from spills.

Hacks to clean kitchen appliances

A modern day kitchen is incomplete without appliances such as a microwave oven, a food processor, a fridge etc. They make life easier, but when it comes to cleaning them, it can be a big headache.

Let's look at hacks and recipes to clean each one in detail.

Food processor

Food processors can be tricky to clean. They have a lot of nooks and crevices, where it is difficult to reach and clean. These places start accumulating food particles that get lodged in them and start to rot. Rotting food starts to develop fungus that can cause stomach upsets.

Tips:-

- The best way of cleaning blender jars is by adding in a little liquid soap along with an equal amount of water and running it for half a minute. The soapy water manages to dislodge all food particles from above and under the blades.

- Wipe the outside of the blender using a mix of vinegar and water. The vinegar helps in removing tough stains.

- The best thing to use to wipe the groove of the machine is mouthwash. Pour a little mouthwash on a sponge and wipe the groove thoroughly. Not only will it prevent any mold from growing but also deodorize the machine.

Microwave oven/OTG

Microwaves and OTG's burden you with a variety of cleaning needs. From burnt bread smell to chicken gravy stains, microwaves need to be thoroughly cleaned in order to get rid of the stains and smells.

Tips:-

- Place a bowl containing equal parts liquid soap and water and run the microwave at highest heat for five minutes. Remove the bowl and wipe the insides of the machine using a sponge. The liquid soap helps in breaking down the gunk and also deodorizing the microwave.
- Place a measuring cup full of water with 4-5 lemon slices. Heat it for around 10 minutes. Remove it and wipe the insides using dryer sheets. Your oven will look shiny and smell fresh.
- Another smart hack is to place around 10 wet tissues inside the oven. The tissues heat up and release a steam that helps in cutting down the grime. This is especially effective in OTG's but be sure to not allow the paper to touch the heating rods, lest they catch fire.
- Simply placing a wet sponge for 5 minutes in an oven and heating it for 15 minutes at low heat will get rid of germs.
- Mix 2 tablespoons of baking powder with enough water to make a thick paste. Use the paste to clean the insides of the oven.

- Mix 50% vinegar and 50% water and use it to clean the glass doors of the ovens.
- Alternately, use a close grain sandpaper to scrap away the food stains on the doors.
- To get rid of the smell of burnt foods, sprinkle kosher salts on a half cut lemon and scrub the insides of the oven.

Recipes

Microwave cleaner I

Ingredients:

- Vinegar
- Lemon juice

Preparation:

1. Take a small cup and pour some vinegar and lemon juice in it. (Exact proportion is not necessary).
2. Put the cup in the microwave/oven and start it. Let it run at medium heat for about 2 minutes. (Do not put any lid on the cup)
3. Unplug the microwave but leave the door closed for about 5 minutes.
4. Open the door and wipe the sides with a sponge or a cloth dipped in warm water. No scrubbing required. This will clean the sides.

Microwave cleaner II
Ingredients:

- Salt
- Vinegar

Preparation

1. Pour vinegar into a spray bottle.
2. Turn the heat in the oven to 260 degrees F (125 C).
3. Once the oven is heated, spray the vinegar solution over the caked-on stuff and let it soak.
4. Pour a thick layer of salt over the stubborn marks.
5. Turn the heat off and let the oven cool. Use a wet towel to scrub away the stains.

Note: You may use baking soda instead of salt. In you do that, let the baking soda stay for some time before scrubbing.

Oven cleaning liquid
Ingredients

- ½ cup liquid soap
- 3 cups baking soda
- 6-8 drops orange or rose essential oil
- 1/2 cup vinegar
- Water as per requirement to make a thick paste

Preparation

1. Mix everything in a bowl and transfer the mixture into a diffuser bottle.

2. Use the liquid for cleaning the oven from the inside and the outside regularly.

Fridge

Refrigerators have become an integral part of our lives. Not only does it keep our veggies, fruits, meat and leftovers fresh, but also give us nice cold ice cubes to go into our drinks. But the fridge gets dirty and stinky in no time, especially after a power cut. Here are some tips to clean the refrigerator.

Tips:-

- Place a small bowl of baking soda inside the fridge and the freezer to take away the 'fridge-y' smells.

- Placing cling wraps or removable plastic mats inside the fridge, atop the different racks, will help in easy cleaning.

- Use natural dish liquid and water to clean the insides of the fridge.

- Make sure you keep the coils behind the fridge dust free. That will not just prevent dust mites from entering the fridge but also help you save on electricity bills.

Dishwasher

Tips:-

- In an empty dishwasher, pour a packet of lemon flavored tang or kool aid or any lemon flavored squash mix. Run the dishwasher for a normal cycle. The dishwasher will become as clean as new and smell fresh.

- Fill two bowls or measuring cups with vinegar and place one on the topmost shelf and one on the bottommost shelf and run the washer at the warmest setting. Wipe the insides of the machine with a dry sponge.

- Use borax powder and water to clean the insides of the dishwasher. After which, sprinkle some borax at the bottom and run the machine. Use a dry sponge to push out the borax.

- Mix ½ cup baking soda with equal parts vinegar and use it to scrub the insides of the oven.

- For a very dirty dishwasher with a lot of stains, place a measuring cup full of hydrogen peroxide (35%) or bleach (optional) and run the washer for 30 minutes.

Recipes

Dishwasher cleaning bombs

Ingredients

- Two cups baking soda

- Three tablespoons hydrogen peroxide (35%)

- 20 drops lavender essential oil

Preparation

1. Mix all ingredients in a glass bowl and make small balls out of the mix.

2. Rest the balls overnight and store them in a jar.

3. To use, place a cup containing vinegar and water and drop a bomb before running on normal cycle.

Dishwasher detergent powder

Ingredients

- 1 cup borax

- 1 cup washing soda

- ½ cup citric acid

- ½ cup salt

Preparation

1. Mix all the ingredients in a glass bowl and store in a glass jar.

2. Use like you would use a normal dish detergent.

Coffee maker

Tips:-

- Mix water with vinegar for cleaning the coffee maker.

- To get rid of the lingering aroma, pour in a cup of white rice and give it a run. The rice will absorb the aroma.

- Alternately, grind a cup of baking soda and wipe the jar clean.

Recipe

Cleaning coffee maker
Ingredients:

- Vinegar
- Water

Preparation:

1. Pour vinegar and water into the coffee maker.
2. For 1 part of vinegar in two parts of water. If the pot of your coffee maker is of 12 cup capacity, fill it till line 4 with the vinegar and then up to the brim with water.
3. Turn the coffee maker on and let it brew. When the brewing cycle is complete, turn the switch off and let the vinegar solution sit for 15 minutes.
4. You do not need to do any scrubbing as this would clean the pot. Simply pour out the vinegar solution.
5. To remove any traces of vinegar, brew the pot twice with plain water. After brewing both the times, let the water sit for 15 minutes.
6. Mix some dishwasher detergent in water and wash the pot in the sink.

Kitchen dust bins

Don't you just hate the drippy mess that garbage bags create, while you transfer them from the kitchen to the dumpster? Cleaning up the watery mess can be both repulsive and painful. Well, here are a few tips to help you solve the problem.

Tips:-

- Make a few newspaper balls and place them at the bottom of the dustbin. Place the dust bin bags on top of the newspaper balls. The balls will effectively soak up all the dirty water and not cause any leaks and stains.

- Make a couple of small holes at the bottom of the dust bin as it will allow for the bad odor to escape.

Utensils

Tips:-

- To get rid of burnt stains pour ½ cup vinegar in half a bucket of warm water and immerse the utensil for half an hour. Remove it and sprinkle baking soda on top and scrub using a kitchen scour. Stains from inside and outside will disappear.

- Another tip is to bring water to a boil in the vessel and throw in a couple of onions cut in half. Allow the water to cool before scrubbing. The stains will disappear.

- Use wood polish to polish the outsides of toasters.

- Cream of tartar works miracles in cleaning stainless steel appliances.

- Use a mix of tamarind paste and salt or lemon and salt to clean copper utensils.

- Use wood ash to clean silverware. Simply scrub silver utensils with a toothbrush dipped in wood ash.

- Use vinegar to shine glassware.

Recipes

Natural soap for dishwashing
Ingredients

- ½ cup castile soap

- 1/8 cup water

- 5 drops of essential oil (lemon preferably)

- 1 teaspoon vinegar

Preparation

1. Mix all the ingredients and transfer into an old liquid dish dispenser.

2. Use a few drops to scrub a tub full of utensils!

Cleaning burnt pot or scorched pan
Ingredients

- 1 cup vinegar
- 2 tablespoons baking soda
- 1 cup water (or depending upon the size of the pan or pot)
- Dishwasher detergent (recipe above)

Instructions

1. Fill the bottom of the pot or pan with a layer of water.

2. Add vinegar to the water.

3. Put the pan on stove and bring the vinegar solution to boil. When some of the grease begins to drop off, turn the stove off.

4. Remove the pan from the stove and add some baking soda to it. This would produce some fizz.

5. Use the detergent to scourge the burnt surface. In case this doesn't work, make a paste of baking soda in a few drops of water. Apply this paste on the stubborn marks and let it stay for some time.

6. Scrub the bottom again. Now the grease should come off easily.

7. Wash with water.

Cast-iron pan cleaner

Ingredients:

- 1 tablespoon olive oil
- 1 teaspoon coarse salt
- hot water

Preparation:

1. Sprinkle the coarse salt in the cast-iron pan.

2. Add a thin layer of olive oil to the inside surface of the pan.

3. Let it stay for a couple of minutes before scrubbing it with a stiff brush.

4. Rinse it off with hot water.

Chapter 4: Living Room/Hall Cleaning Hacks

Ah, living rooms! Places where guests are entertained and families gather to have a good time. Where kitty parties are played out and sports nights are enjoyed. Living rooms are where we spend most of our lives, so maintaining a clean and neat living room is extremely important. The four main areas that need cleaning include couches, carpet, floor and ceiling/walls/windows.

Hacks for cleaning couches

Leather, polyester, white, brown; no matter what the color and type of couch you have, they all need a good scrub from time to time.

Tips:-

- For old leather couches that have discolored, use shoe polish to polish them. It helps in adding back shine and also helps in getting rid of scratches and scruffs.

- Mix 50% vinegar and 50% cold water and spray the mixture over leather couch stains. The mix will also help in getting rid of water stains.

- While cleaning fabric couches, it is better to use as little water as possible. Water that gets trapped in between the layers can develop a mold, which can cause the couch to stink.

- If there are dried up stains like food gravy stains then use a pumice stone to scrub it away.

- For white and cream couches, use a mix of lemon juice and salt to rub over stains. The process will also whiten and brighten the couches.

Recipes for cleaners

Fabric cleaner

Ingredients

- ¼ cup vinegar

- ¾ cup water

- ½ tablespoon dish liquid

Preparation

1. Transfer all the ingredients into a plastic spray bottle.

2. Spray the couches with the mix and scrub using a sponge dipped in warm water.

3. Wipe with a dry cloth to get rid of the water stains.

Fabric refresher

Ingredients

- ¼ cup baking soda

- 10 drops essential oils

- Water

- Spray bottle

Preparation

1. Transfer all the soda and water into a spray bottle and give it a good mix.

2. Add in the essential oil and shake the bottle

3. Use the spray to get rid of damp and wet smell from couches.

All purpose furniture cleaner
Ingredients

- ¾ cup water

- 1 tablespoon olive oil

- 2 tablespoon vodka

- 2 tablespoon vinegar

- 40 drops essential oils (lavender, orange, eucalyptus etc.)

- 1 tablespoon glycerin

- ½ teaspoon beeswax

Preparation

1. Pour the water, oil, vodka, vinegar, glycerin and essential oil in a mixer jar and whiz till everything is nicely mixed up.

2. Open the dropper lid and pour in the beeswax.

3. Pour the mix into a spray bottle.

4. Use to clean, couches, carpets, polish wooden furniture etc.

Bug spray
Ingredients

- 2 tablespoons borax

- 1 cup vinegar

- 40 drops eucalyptus oil

- 20 drops neem oil

Preparation

1. Mix all the ingredients and fill up a spray bottle.

2. Spray in sofa crevices, underside of tables, on window grills.

3. The mix is extremely effective in killing ants, bugs, fleas and those dreaded dog ticks.

Furniture polisher

Ingredients

- 1 lemon

- 1 cup olive oil (mineral oil)

- 1 cup vinegar

Preparation

1. Mix all the ingredients and place in a spray bottle.

2. Use to polish tables, chairs, cabinets, sofa handles etc.

Hacks for cleaning carpets

Nothing like a fresh clean carpet to make you feel at home! Carpets need regular cleaning and having them professionally cleaned can turn out to be quite an expensive affair. There are also the dangers of them using heavy duty chemicals, which can be harmful for health, with children and pets being at most risk. Here are a few tips to help you keep your carpets clean and free from dust.

Tips:-

- To clean carpets, use a mixture of 1 cup vinegar with 10 drops lavender essential oil added in. The vinegar will thoroughly clean the carpet and the essential oil will get rid of any bad odor.

- Using eucalyptus instead of lavender will help in keeping insects such as fleas, mosquitoes and bed bugs at bay.

- To get rid of the dreadful animal hair, use a squeegee to run over the entire length of the carpet. The squeegee will pull away all of the hair and render the carpet hair/fur free.

- Sprinkle talcum powder over vomit and allow it to soak all of it up. Simply vacuum the powder and wash the surface using vinegar. To prevent the vacuum from smelling, drop in a ball of cotton that's been soaked in a few drops of essential oil. The ball of cotton will dissipate a nice odor.

- Use a mix of 2 parts water to 1 part vodka, to get rid of tough stains.

- For dried up stains, use a clothing brush to scrub away the stain.

- Another great tip is to pour a little milk over the carpet stain and rub a half cut lemon on top. The curdling process helps in dislodging the stain.

- Use rubbing alcohol to get rid of nail polish stains.

- To get rid of hard stains, pour some vodka or rubbing alcohol over it. Allow it to stand for about 10 minutes. Place a baking paper on top and place a hot iron. The stain will get stuck to the paper. Lift it gently.

Recipes for cleaning solutions

Carpet stain remover
Ingredients

- ½ cup Baking soda

- ½ cup Vinegar

- ½ cup Dish liquid

Preparation

1. Mix all the ingredients and transfer into a spray bottle Spray a little amount over the stain and allow it to stand for some time. Use a wet sponge to wipe off the mix along with the stain.

Alternately, dip a mop into the mix and wipe it over the carpet for general stain removal.

You can even use club soda instead of the vinegar and baking soda. Just use 1 cup of soda mixed with ½ cup vinegar and ½ cup water. The subsequent liquid will be very effective in removing stains.

Carpet freshener

Ingredients

- 2 cups borax

- 1 cup baking soda

- 40 drops essential oils (strawberry, rose, lemon etc.)

Preparation

1. Mix borax with baking soda and essential oil in a glass bowl.

2. Allow the mixture to mature for 24-48 hours.

3. To use, sprinkle the mix over carpet and either vacuum it or wipe with a sponge.

Hacks for cleaning ceilings/ceiling fans/walls/windows

Tips:-

- Use balloons to clear cobwebs on ceilings. Smear a little baby oil on top of a helium balloon. Secure the balloon with a string and let it float toward the ceiling. Guide it towards the cobwebs and maneuver it to dislodge the web. Pull the balloon down and wipe the web using a cloth. Repeat.

- To remove oil or grease stains from walls, rub a piece of chalk over it. Make sure that every inch of the stain is covered and is thick enough to easily come off. Wait for five minutes before using a damp sponge or cloth to take it off.

- One of the best hacks to clean a ceiling fan is to place an old unused pillow cover over one of its blades and pulling it such that all the dirt and dust gets collected inside the case. The case can then be taken outside and jerked to get rid of the dust and used for the rest of the blades. Just make sure that it's an old pillow cover, as using it again might cause respiratory problems.

- For wallpapers that have balls of dust and dirt and are old and sticky, use the soft center of fresh bread to take them off. You can also use the center of a freshly baked bagel. Sounds strange, but it's really effective.

- To remove grease stains from wallpapers, hold a tissue or blotting paper over the stain and press a hot iron over it. The iron will slowly dissolve the stain and the paper will absorb the grease. Make sure you wear oven mittens and then hold the paper to avoid getting burnt. Do not press the iron directly on the wallpaper as that can damage it.

- Lemon essential oil is a boon for parents with toddlers in their houses. Crayon marks on walls and furniture can be a big headache to clean, but simply dabbing a little lemon oil over the stain and lightly rubbing using a wet cloth will make the stain disappear. The oil can be used to get rid of ink and pencil marks as well.

- To remove scruff marks from walls, apply a thin coat of toothpaste (white paste not gel) and use a soft bristled toothbrush to move in a circular motion.

- Use a lint roller to get rid of dust from lamp shades.

- Use a bottle of compressed air to blow out dust and dirt from exhaust fans.

- Use a butter knife and cloth to clean between ventilator panels.

- To clean dirty windows mix together 1 tablespoon ammonia, 3 tablespoons rubbing alcohol and 1 liter warm water and use a sponge to dip and wipe the windows.

- Dip a sponge in any oil and rub over the grills to get rid of rust.

- To get rid of dust from candles, place them in a pair of old tights and give them a good shake. The candles will be as good as new.

- Use q-tips to clean between window sills. Pour a little vinegar to help dislodge sticky dirt and rain stains.

Recipes for cleaners

Wall stain remover

Ingredients

- ½ cup vinegar

- 1 cup ammonia

- ¼ cup baking soda

- 1 gallon warm water

Preparation

1. Mix all the ingredients together in a large enough bucket.

2. Apply the mixture onto the walls using a sponge and scrub until all the stains come off.

3. The mixture can be applied to any colored wall since it will not dull the color.

4. Wear rubber gloves when using this mixture, since ammonia can cause damage to your skin. Also, make sure that all windows and doors are open to allow the smell to escape.

Hacks for cleaning floors

For people who do not have carpets in their living rooms, the floor single handedly has to bear the brunt of all types of walking, running, spilling and breaking activities. That keeps it from gleaming and takes away some of the beauty of the room. Here are tips to keep your floors nice and shiny.

Marble floors

- Use a mix of 50% castile soap and 50% water to clean and shine marble floors.

- Mop the stains with lemon juice and olive oil and wipe the floor using a chamois cloth.

- Sprinkle corn starch over an oil stain and allow it to absorb the grease. Wipe it off using a damp cloth.

- For tough stains on light colored marble, pour some hydrogen peroxide over the stain and place plastic wrap over it. Allow it to remain for 24 hours before scrubbing it using a wet sponge.

- An alternate method is applying a mix of water and baking soda over the stain and curing it for 24 hours with a food wrap covering. Wipe it using a damp sponge.

- For paint stains, use a fine grain sandpaper to gently scrap away the stains.

Granite floors

- One of the best ways to prevent granite from losing its shine is to wipe it using distilled warm water.

- To remove stains, apply a thin coat of acetone and scrub the area using utensil scrubber.

- To polish granite floors, mix baking soda and water with a 1 is to 3 ratio. Mop the floor using the mix.

- Alternately, mix 1 part rubbing alcohol to 3 parts water and mop the floor.

Recipes for wooden floor cleaners

Wood floor polisher
Ingredients

- 4 liters hot water

- ¾ cup olive oil

- ½ cup lemon juice

Preparation

- Mix all ingredients in a bucket and use to mop wooden floors.

- The lemon helps in getting stains off and the oil renders the floor shiny.

Floor disinfectant
Ingredients

- 4 liters hot water

- ¼ cup borax

- 5 drops eucalyptus oil

- 5 drops peppermint oil

- 5 drops lavender oil

Preparation

1. Mix all the ingredients in a bucket and mop the floors using the mix.

2. The borax kills all ants and ant eggs and the peppermint and eucalyptus oils deter mice.

Hacks for cleaning computer/laptops

Tips:-

- To clean keyboards, use a soft tooth brush or make up brush.

- Use a small towel dipped in rubbing alcohol, to clean computer screens.

- Use a can of compressed air to blast dirt out of computer speakers.

- Use q-tips to rub rubbing alcohol over earbuds/ear phones. The alcohol will kill germs.

Chapter 5: Bedroom Cleaning Hacks

Clean and neat bedrooms will allow you to have a good night's sleep and will help take away your stress. When you say bedroom, the most essential element in there is a bed and a wardrobe. Here are tips and hacks to keep your beds and wardrobes clean.

Hacks for cleaning the wardrobe
Tips:-

- To get ink stains off of your clothes sprinkle some baking soda and rub a lemon on it. The stain will fade away. The same technique can be used to lighten armpit stains on shirts.

- Alternately, use a mix of hydrogen peroxide and baking soda to get rid of armpit stains on shirts and dresses.

- To clean the bottom of canvas/converse shoes mix 1 tablespoon each of baking soda, vinegar and hot water and use a toothbrush to scrub away the stains. Toothpaste will also work equally well.

- To make cupboards smell nice drop in a bar of freshly opened soap in a drawer or place under a pile of clothes.

- To keep your jeans looking new without washing it frequently...just pop those in the freezer to kill odor causing bacteria and your jeans will be as good as new!

- A mix of 50% vinegar and 50% water can help colored clothes from bleeding. Dark clothes that run color can be soaked in the mixture for half an hour.

- If you haven't washed a dress and have to wear it urgently then just spray vodka on it. That will remove any sweat and other bad odors.

- To remove lipstick stains from clothes just spray hair spray on it. That will easily remove the stain.

- Use a nail file to file away dirt from suede shoes.

- Polish leather shoes with your body moisturizer to lend it a shine.

- Another tip is to use glass cleaner to clean leather jackets and boots. Use a small amount and use tissue papers to rub the boots.

- Place a small amount of baking soda in a small piece of tissue inside you sneaker to absorb sweat smell.

- To remove wine stains from clothing, pour white wine on the stained area and allow it to stand for about 5 minutes. Wash off the white wine using a strong detergent.

- Use a mixture of 2/3 cup ammonia, 6 tablespoons baking soda and 2 cups warm water to get tough stains off of clothes.

- Add ½ cup hydrogen peroxide (35%) ½ cup washing soda and 1 cup warm water to a bucket of water and soak clothes in it overnight. All tough stains will vanish.

- Soak baby clothes overnight in half a bucket of water containing 1 cup baking soda. The soda will remove stains and help kill bacteria. No detergents need to be used thus keeping baby skin safe.

- To get stains off an iron, just sprinkle some salt over the ironing board and heat up the iron to its highest setting. Gently press it over the salt and hold for 5 minutes. The stain will stick to the salt.

- Use a small ball of steel wool to clean curling rods. Hair straighteners can also be cleaned with steel wool.

- Use toothpaste to clean and add sheen to engagement rings.

Hacks for cleaning the bedding

- To get wet urine stains out of a mattress sprinkle borax over it and allow it to dry for 24 hours under the sun. Dust away or vacuum the powder.

- To get rid of moisture, simply pour sea salt over it and allow it to absorb the moisture. The trick also helps in absorbing stain causing spills, such as coffees and red wine.

- Simply rubbing a mix of baking soda and lemon over the stain will help in getting rid of mattress stains

- To get rid of the damp smell, pour a mix of vodka and lemon and allow it to dry in the sun.

- Mix 10 drops of clove oil and 10 drops of eucalyptus oil in ½ cup of water and pour into a spray bottle. Spray the mattress, under the bed and around the bed to get rid of dust mites and bed bugs.

- Use play-doh to pick up glitter and pieces of glass.

Recipes for cleaners

All purpose mattress cleaner
Ingredients

- 8.1 oz (240 ml) hydrogen peroxide (35%)

- 2 teaspoon dish washing liquid

- 2 or 3 tablespoons baking soda

Preparation

1. Mix all the ingredients and pour into a spray bottle.

2. Spray the liquid all over the mattress and wipe with a dry sponge.

3. All stains including urine stains will easily come off.

Mattress/sheets spray

Ingredients

- 1 teaspoon lavender essential oil

- ¼ cup vodka

- 4 cups water

Preparation

1. Mix all the ingredients and pour into a spray bottle.

2. Spray the mattress and sheets regularly to get rid of bad odors.

Chapter 5: DIY For Your Garden (Bonus Chapter)

Another area where the entire family loves to relax and de-stress is the garden. Maintaining the garden can be a pain if you don't take extra care. Here are some tips you undertake to maintain a clean garden area.

Tips:-

- To avoid the hassle of nursery beds, simply plant your saplings in egg shells. Then throw the shells inside the pot. They will degrade and provide the plant with extra nutrition.

- Mix 10 drops of neem oil with 1 tablespoon soap powder and place inside a spray bottle. Add in a liter of water and spray over plants. The mix will keep bugs and other insects at bay and also kill insect eggs.

- Always store fertilizers in plastic containers, especially coco-peat. The moisture from the peat can make cardboard boxes soggy and might create a mess over time.

- Place plates below each and every pot to help prevent water from flowing everywhere. You can also place balls of paper to help soak up the water and prevent stagnation.

- To clean gardening tools immerse them in a tub of warm water containing vinegar.

- Use linseed oil to polish the wooden handles of gardening tools.

- Kill weeds using vinegar. Simply spray vinegar on plant roots and the plant on a whole to kill them and prevent them from growing again.

That's all, folks!

I hope that these recipes and tips will help you as much as they helped me.

Finally, if you enjoyed this book, could you please take a moment to share your thoughts and post a review on Amazon?
It would be greatly appreciated as your feedback will encourage me to create more books for you to enjoy!

Thank You again for your interest in my work!
Annette Goodman

Shopping List/Index

Here's a list of all the products mentioned in this book:

- Ammonia

- Baking powder/baking soda

- Hydrogen peroxide - 35% and 3% concentration solution.

- Vinegar

- Lemons

- Grapefruits

- Onions

- Essential oils (lemon, orange, lavender, rose, peppermint, eucalyptus, black pepper - to your smell).

- Olive oil

- Baby oil

- Oil spray

- Neem oil

- Mineral oil

- Castile soap

- Kosher salt

- Natural liquid soap (the less chemicals, the better).

- Mouthwash

- Rubbing alcohol

- Vodka

- Grain sandpaper

- Cola

- Tang/Kool-Aid

- Borax

- Cream of Tartar

- Bleach

- Tamarind paste

- Toothbrush

- Wood Ash

- Pumice Stone

- Scrub Brush

- Glycerin

- Beeswax

- Talcum powder

- Cotton balls

- Chalk

- Blotting paper

- Paper tissues

- Lint roller

- Q-tips

- Chamois cloth

- Mirror/glass polishing cloth

- Corn starch

- Distilled water

- Acetone

- Steel wool

- Vegetable glycerin

- Liquid castile soap

- Antibacterial essential oil

- Distilled water

- Isopropyl (rubbing) alcohol

- Cling wraps

- Plastic bags and rubber bands

Recommended Reading For You:

You may also want to check my other books:

-> Anti Inflammatory Diet: Beginner's Guide: What You Need To Know To Heal Yourself with Food + Recipes + One Week Diet Plan

"He who takes medicine and neglects to diet wastes the skill of his doctors." -Chinese Proverb

Are you suffering from the severe symptoms that you've been trying to overcome for a long time now using your prescribed pills, but just stuck somewhere in the middle?

Unrestrained inflammation lead to asthma, allergies, tissue and cell degeneration, heart diseases, cancer and various other maladies, which are difficult to deal with.
I myself suffered from long and gruesome periods of acute inflammation. I had IBS symptoms and very bad, extremely painful sinusitis. It started to affect my day-to-day ability to work, and my potential and productivity suffered a steep decline. Medication helped, but the effect was only temporary. The fact that I was slightly overweight did not help either. I would be confined to my house for days without any solution to my problem. Every doctor I visited could pinpoint the superficial problem and treat it, time after time, but none could tell me what was causing this problem.

And the problem was my diet!

Vast majority of the recipes I included in this book can be prepared really fast and easily! I also included absolutely delicious One Week Diet Plan for you!

->Direct Buy Link: http://www.amazon.com/dp/B00MQ9HI58/

->Paperback Version: https://www.createspace.com/4974692

-> Fast Freezer Meals: 46 Delicious and Quick Gluten-Free Slow Cooker Recipes for Make-Ahead Meals That Will Save Your Time and Improve Your Health

Discover Delicious and Quick Gluten-Free Slow Cooker Recipes for Make-Ahead Meals That Will Save Your Time and Improve Your Health!

As a busy businesswoman, wife and mom I know exactly how hard it is to prepare healthy and tasty meals for me and my family every day, especially when they have to be gluten-free! **See yourself that gluten-diet doesn't have to be bland, and home cooking doesn't have to be time-consuming!**

Most of these recipes can be prepared in no more than 30 minutes and then just effortlessly cooked in your crockpot when you're at work or doing your business!
-I included a shopping list inside to **save your precious time.**
-No matter if you are gluten intolerant or not – **these meals are**

delicious, healthy and suitable for everyone!

-In this book you will also find **freezing and thawing safety guide.**

These recipes will enrich your culinary experience and let you **save massive time!**

->Direct Buy Link: http://www.amazon.com/dp/B00M783PS2/

->Paperback Version:

https://www.createspace.com/4944068

-> Gluten Free Crock Pot Recipes: Healthy, Easy and Delicious Slow Cooker Paleo Recipes for Breakfast, Lunch and Dinner

Discover Healthy, Easy and Delicious Slow Cooker Paleo Recipes for Breakfast, Lunch and Dinner for You and Your Family!

Save your time and start healthy living with these delectable slow cooker gluten free recipes tailor-made for busy people!

I've been on the Gluten Free diet for more than ten years now! Although the main reason for my radical diet change was my diagnosis (Coeliac disease), **I would never-ever (even if given a magical chance) take the lane of eating gluten again.** The Gluten Free diet will help you **detoxify, lose extra weight, minimize catching colds/getting sick too often and feel younger - both mentally and physically.**

->Direct Buy Link: http://www.amazon.com/dp/B00K5UVYUA/

->Paperback Version:

https://www.createspace.com/4823966

-> **Gluten-Free Vegan Cookbook: 90+ Healthy, Easy and Delicious Recipes for Vegan Breakfasts, Salads, Soups, Lunches, Dinners and Desserts for Your Well-Being**

Discover Healthy, Easy and Delicious Gluten-Free Vegan Recipes for You and Your Family!

Gluten-Free Vegan diet doesn't have to be bland and boring at all! These recipes are original, easy to make and just delightfully appetizing. They will enrich your culinary experience and let you enjoy your breakfasts, lunches, dinners and desserts with your friends and family.

Start living healthy today! I've Included a Shopping List Inside to Save Your Precious Time!

No matter what are your reasons to follow vegan, gluten-free or both of these diets, this book will provide you with many great cooking ideas that me and my family developed during our gluten-free years.

In this book you will find:

-23 Scrumptious and Easy Breakfasts

-27 Delicious and Savory Lunches and Dinners

-22 Aromatic And Nutritious Soups

-21 Enticing And Rich Desserts

-Extra Shopping List to Save Your Precious Time

= 93 Fantastic Gluten-Free Healthy Vegan Recipes!

->Direct Buy Link: http://www.amazon.com/dp/B00LU915YA/

->Paperback Version:
https://www.createspace.com/4907669

-> Paleo Smoothie Recipes: 67 Delicious Paleo Smoothies For Weight Loss And a Healthy Lifestyle – Annette Goodman

67 Easy and Fast Delicious Smoothie Recipes for Effective Weight Loss and Sexy Body!

Kill the food cravings and get in shape with these delicious and healthy Paleo Smoothies!

In This Book I'll Show You:

-Why Paleo Smoothies are great for Weight Loss (and Weight Maintenance!)
-67 Tasty Paleo Recipes great for Weight Loss, Detox, and keeping your body Healthy every day!
-How to make the Paleo approach easier!
-Important facts about some of the ingredients you'd like to know.
-Planning and Directions – how to get started fast!
-How to maintain your motivation, finally lose the extra pounds and be happy with a Sexy Body!

->Direct Buy Link:
http://www.amazon.com/dp/B00J8ZHMIQ/

->Paperback Version:

https://www.createspace.com/4803901

-> Low Carb Slow Cooker: 50 Delicious and Easy Crock Pot Recipes for Rapid Weight Loss

If you often find yourself confused about how to whip up a yummy dish for a low-carb diet, this book is just the perfect thing you need right now.

The recipes mentioned in this book are not only simple but they require every day ingredients from your kitchen.
Food tastes best when you cook it with some love. Nothing can beat the mouth-watering dishes that can be cooked in a Crockpot.
Start Losing Weight Effectively and For Good!

The Recipes In This Book Will Come in Handy When You Find Yourself Pressed For Time.
There are as many as 50 different recipes that will make your life easier when you are on a low-carb diet program. While your food is getting cooked in the Crockpot, you can go catch your favorite movie or put your feet up and curl up in your bed.
A low carb diet will seem so much easier to follow when you have yummy food to go with it.
It will almost feel like you are having a cheat meal each day.

In This Book You Will Read About:

-What is Low Carb Diet?
-Who Should Use it And Who Should Not?
-Pros and Properties of Low Carb Diet
-Debunking Some Common Myths
-Best and Worst Food Choices You Can Make
-Foods You Need to Avoid

-Important Tips and Advice
-10 Low-carb Slow-Cooker Aromatic Soups Recipes
-11 Low-carb Crockpot Delicious Chicken recipes
-10 Low-carb Slow-cooker Amazingly Good Sea-food
-10 Low-carb slow-cooker Yummy Pork Recipes
-9 Low-carb Slow-cooker Scrumptious Lamb Recipes

->**Direct Buy Link: http://www.amazon.com/dp/B00O2AACR0/**

->**Paperback Version:**

https://www.createspace.com/5042178

My Mailing list: If you would like to **receive new Kindle reads** on **weight loss, wellness, diets, recipes and healthy living** for FREE I invite you to my Mailing List. Whenever my new book is out, I set the free period for two days. You will get an e-mail notification and will **be the first to get the book for $0** during its limited promotion.

Why would I do this when it took me countless hours to write these e-books?

First of all, that's my way of saying **"thank you"** to my new readers. Second of all – **I want to spread the word about my new books and ideas.** Mind you that **I hate spam and e-mails that come too frequently** - no worries about that.

If you think that's a good idea and are in, just follow this link:

http://eepurl.com/6elQD

You can also follow us on Facebook:

www.facebook.com/HolisticWellnessBooks

We have created this page with a few fellow authors of mine. We hope you find it inspiring and helpful.

Thank You for your time and interest in our work!

Annette Goodman & Holistic Wellness Books

About The Author

Hello! My name is Annette Goodman.

I'm glad we met. Who am I?

A homegrown cook, successful wellness aficionado and a writer. I live in Portland, Oregon with my husband, son and our dear golden retriever, Fluffy. I work as a retail manager in of the European companies.

My entire childhood I suffered from obesity, hypertension and complexion problems. During my college years I decided to turn my life around and started my weight-loss and wellness pursue. After more than a decade I can say that I definitely succeeded and now I'd like to give you a hand.

I love creating new healthy recipes, cooking and writing books about healthy lifestyle for you to enjoy and profit from.

I hope we'll meet again!

You can visit my Amazon Author Page:

http://www.amazon.com/Annette-Goodman/e/B00LLPE1QM/

Printed in Great Britain
by Amazon

39680844R00050